Soulmate Manifestation Goals Ideas

Single/divorced/widowed?
Age range?
Income/money/home/vehicle?
Ideal astrology sign/s?
Personality:
funny/serious/outgoing/quiet/kind/cheerful/adventurous/intellectual/affectionate/easygoing/thoughtful/sociable/homebody/generous/creative/loyal/successful/dependable/romantic/modest/religious/political/moral/tidy/healthy/introvert/extrovert?
Career/Job:
 doctor/veterinarian/dentist/writer/musician/psychologist/entrepreneur/lawyer/farmer/sports/carer/healer/pilot/sailor/chef/shopkeeper/hotelier/military/driver/surgeon/waiter/gardener/cook/managerial/fitness/teacher/artist/singer/writer/animals/engineer/administrator/manufacturer/politician?
Health condition/any acceptable illnesses?
Children? Pets? Friends? Family?
Taste in music, books, films, TV programs?
Hobbies/interests/sports/social media/gardening?
Clothes/style/hair type and color?
Build/weight/height/fitness?
Hairstyle/facial hair?
Glasses/contact lenses?
Nationality/town/culture/accent/languages?

We really hope you get everything you ever wish for and more. Thank you for buying this book and for the connection between us. Please leave a review or rating if it's no problem. You can also please check our other books and follow us for more.
https://www.treehouse-books.net/